Story Masks for Fairy Tales

by
Gwenn Jones Rives

illustrated by
Darcy Meyers

Publishers
T.S. Denison & Company, Inc.
Minneapolis, Minnesota 55431

Standard Book Number: 513-02097-7
Story Masks for Fairy Tales
Copyright © 1992 by the T.S. Denison & Company, Inc.
Minneapolis, Minnesota 55431

Story Masks for Fairy Tales
Introduction

Story Masks for Fairy Tales brings you language arts experiences through the telling and retelling of nine of the best-loved fairy tales. For each of the stories you are provided a teacher's guide page featuring a multitude of whole language activities, followed by the enchantingly illustrated story character masks. *Story Masks for Fairy Tales* will quickly become a treasured resource for enhancing the development of expressive, receptive and written language skills.

1. Read the story aloud to your class. Fluency and expression are keys to generating excitement and comprehension.

2. Retell the story using the story masks at your face to model the dramatic presentation.

3. Have the students retell the story with your guidance. Hold up the story masks to help the students remember characters and sequence.

4. Have the students dramatize the story. Students hold their own mask and provide their own dialogue and movements. Sometimes a narrator enhances the dramatization. Repeat to allow everyone the opportunity to participate.

5. Listen to a tape recording of the story and follow along with the text.

6. Video-tape the dramatiztion with the story masks. Let the students take turns taking the video-tape home overnight to share with their families.

7. Story masks are very mobile. Use them to tell stories to other classrooms, the principal, other school staff members.

8. Provide a few masks from several different stories to encourage students to create new stories. Record the new stories on a cassette tape recorder, and write them down. The possibilities with new stories are endless. Examples: "The Day the Giant met Red Riding Hood's Wolf," "The Ugly Duckling Visits The Beast's Castle," "The Gingerbread Man Moves In With The Three Little Pigs." The children will delight in creating new fairy tales.

9. Have the students paint different scenes from the story and write the narrative underneath. Combine the paintings into a big book for the class.

10. Keep a class journal of the stories that have been dramatized. Record students' reactions. Those students who are not yet able to write can be encouraged to draw pictures for the journal.

Contents

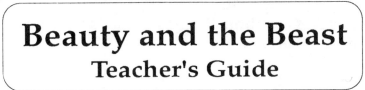

Beauty and the Beast
Teacher's Guide

Exploring the Story

1. Discussion starters:
   - When Beauty's father left to meet his ship, what did Beauty ask for?
   - How was Beauty different from her sisters?
   - How did Beauty's father meet the Beast?
   - Why did Beauty go to the Beast?
   - How did Beauty feel about the Beast?
   - How did the Beast feel about Beauty?
   - What did Beauty promise the Beast?
   - Did she keep her promise?

2. Brainstorm words that describe Beauty and words that describe the Beast. Write two charts. How are they alike and how are they different?

   Beauty is _pretty_ .   Beast is _ugly_ .

   Beauty is _kind_ .   Beast is _kind_ .

   Beauty is _thoughtful_ .   Beast is _thoughtful_ .

   Beauty is _considerate_ .   Beast is _considerate_ .

   Beauty is _lovable_ .   Beast is _generous_ .

3. Create your own chants. Write them on charts and chant frequently. Sentence strips can be made for visual matching or sequencing. Words can be written on cards to be put in order on a wall or pocket chart.

   Example: Beauty is pretty on the outside.
   Beauty is pretty on the inside.
   She's so nice, she's so kind,
   She's so very nice and kind.

   Beast is ugly on the outside.
   Beast is pretty on the inside.
   He's so nice, he's so kind,
   He's so very nice and kind.

4. Discuss how Beast is beautiful. Brainstorm all the ways that people can be beautiful complete this sentence:

I am beautiful _when I share_ .

I am beautiful _when I help others_ .

I am beautiful _sometimes_ .

I am beautiful _when I am kind_ .

I am beautiful _when I try my best_ .

Make a book entitled, "Beautiful (your name)."

a. Tape together two pieces of 6" x 9" poster board leaving 1/8" space between the two pieces.

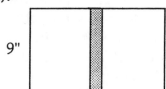

b. Cut wallpaper 11" x 141/8" (1" larger all around). Place posterboard on top.

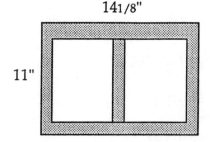

c. Fold down the corners first, then turn down all the edges.

d. Take six pages of 81/2" x 11" paper and fold them in half. Use a long-arm stapler and staple on the fold.

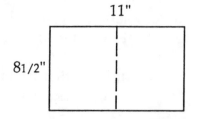

e. Open the first and last pages of the book and glue to the cover. (Rubber cement works well.)

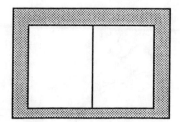

7

10

12

13

Jack and the Beanstalk
Teacher's Guide

Exploring the Story

1. Discussion starters:
   - Did Jack make a good trade for his cow?
   - Was the Giant's wife hospitable to Jack?
   - Why did Jack steal?
   - What would you have done if you were Jack?
   - What are some words to describe the Giant?

2. Encourage the children to write couplets.

   Example: Fe, Fi, Fo, Fum,   Fe, Fi, Fo, Fum,
             I smell grape gum!   I hurt my thumb!

             Fe, Fi, Fo, Fum,   Fe, Fi, Fo, Fum,
             I sing and hum.   I hear him come.

3. Which would you rather have, and why: a bag of gold, a hen that lays golden eggs, or a singing harp? Discuss with the students, tally their opinions, and graph the results.

4. Write a biography about the Giant. Here are some ideas to get you started: name, where he lives, family, favorite foods, hobbies, appearance, likes, dislikes, favorite music. Have the students write autobiographies as a comparison. Students who are not yet able to write can create a pictorial biography in an accordian book by illustrating each page and having the teacher write a caption. *(See next page for directions.)*

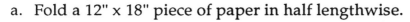

ACCORDION BOOK:

a. Fold a 12" x 18" piece of paper in half lengthwise.

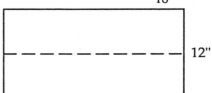

18"

12"

b. Fold in half again crosswise.

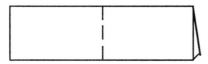

c. Fold ends into center.

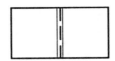

d. Open up the paper and cut half lengthwise.

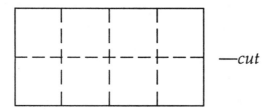

—cut

e. Tape the two pieces together to form one long piece.

tape

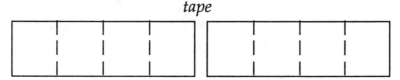

f. Refold back and forth. Illustrate and enjoy!

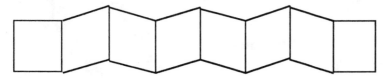

5. Plant bean seeds and record how quickly they grow. Experiment with restricting light and water to see how much these factors affect growth. Speculate about how Jack's beanstalk was different.

17

18

19

21

23

24

The Three Little Pigs
Teacher's Guide

Exploring the Story

1. Discussion starters:
   - Which house was the sturdiest?
   - Why did the wolf want to go inside the pigs' houses?
   - What materials were used to make the houses?
   - Why did the pigs make their houses out of different materials?

2. The refrain can be put on a wall chart for choral reading. These same phrases can be put on sentence strips for visual matching or sequencing. Words can be written on cards to be put in order on a wall or pocket chart.

| Little pig, little pig, | | Little | pig | , | little | pig | , |

| Let me come in. | | Let | me | come | in | . |

3. Discuss wolves as being dangerous animals. Have the students discuss things they are afraid of and write them on a chart. *(Matt is afraid of the dark, Maria is afraid of snakes, etc.)* Read and reread the chart together. Make a class book. Each student may contribute a page by writing and illustrating, "I'm am afraid of..."

4. Discuss the story and brainstorm some different endings:
   - What if the third pig had let the wolf in the house?
   - What if the first pig had built a house of bricks?
   - What if the three pigs had lived together?

   Have the students create their own ending to the story and write it in a book. Each page of the book could be shaped like a pig. *(A sample is provided on the following page.)*

5. Brainstorm words to describe pigs, wolves, and houses. Create your own chants. Examples:

Fat pigs	_Big_ wolves	_Straw_ houses
Smart pigs	_Bad_ wolves	_Stick_ houses
Pink pigs	_Clever_ wolves	_Big_ houses
Dirty pigs	_Hungry_ wolves	_Brick_ houses
We see pigs.	We see wolves.	We see houses.

6. Have the students pretend that they are the Big, Bad Wolf and write to each of the three little pigs inviting them to a barbeque in their honor.

7. Discuss what homes are made of in your community. Graph all the different types of building materials.

LITTLE PIG WRITING PAPER PATTERN

Story Masks for Fairy Tales

28

30

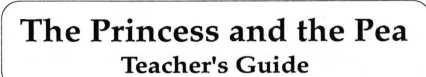

The Princess and the Pea
Teacher's Guide

Exploring the Story

1. Discussion starters:
   - Why did the Princess knock on the Prince's door?
   - Why did the Queen suggest twenty mattresses?
   - Would you be able to feel a pea under your mattress?
   - Could this story have really happened?

2. Experiment: UNDER WHAT THICKNESS CAN YOU FEEL A PEA?

   Materials: dried pea, tissue, napkin, scarf, paper towel, dish towel, bath towel, blanket, sleeping bag, another scarf to be used as a blindfold.

   Procedure: have the students:
   - *Predict (guess)* under which item they will be able to find the pea.
   - *Experiment (do)* Blindfold a student. Place a pea under a tissue, and let the student determine if it can be felt. Repeat with all objects.
   - *Observe (watch)* what happens.
   - *Conclude (discuss)* what happened.
   - *Document (write)* the results on a chart.

3. How can you tell if a princess is real? Brainstorm ideas to complete this sentence:
   A real princess would . . .

   ```
   (wear a crown)
   (be sweet)
   (be kind)
   (be pretty)
   (tell you)
   (grant wishes)
   ```

4. How high is twenty mattresses on top of each other? Have the students measure the thickness of their mattress at home and determine the height of the Princess' bed.

5. Create your own chants. Write them on charts and chant frequently. Sentence strips can be made for visual matching or sequencing. Words can be written on cards to be put in order on a wall or pocket chart.

    example: Tell me how that could be -
                The Princess felt the pea
                Under twenty mattresses
                She felt that tiny pea!

6. If the students have penpals, have them write to their "pals" about this story. If they don't have penpals, try to organize a penpal school program. Penpals could be students in another class, a different school, or undergraduate students from a College of Education.

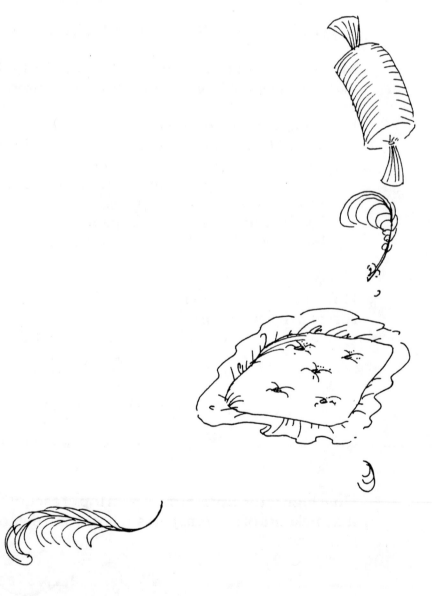

33

34

35

Story Masks for Fairy Tales

37

The Ugly Duckling
Teacher's Guide

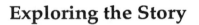

Exploring the Story

1. Discussion starters:
   • The "ugly" duckling was not ugly, but different from the rest of the ducklings. Have you ever felt different from others?
   • Have you ever been left out or not included? How did it feel?
   • How did the other animals treat the "ugly" duckling?
   • How did the "ugly" duckling feel?

2. Compare *The Ugly Duckling* with *Cinderella* (written by the same author, Hans Christian Anderson) and *Rudolph, the Red-Nosed Reindeer*. How are these stories alike and how are they different? Write a similiar story.

3. If you could give the story a different title, what would it be? Brianstorm and write down all your ideas on a chart.

4. Create your own chants. Write them on charts and chant frequently. Sentence strips can be made for visual matching or sequencing. Words can be written down on cards to be put in order on a wall or pocket chart. Look up "cygnet" with the children in a dictionary.

     Example: A beautiful cygnet
                        will never be a duck
                        even with a lot of luck!

                        A beautiful swan
                        is what it will be
                        and swim around for all to see.

40

41

42

43

45

46

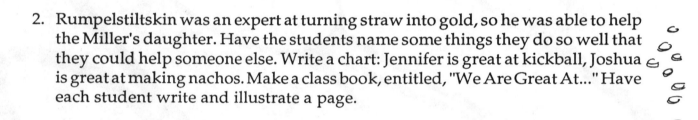

Rumpelstiltskin
Teacher's Guide

Exploring the Story

1. Discussion starters:
    - Is it possible to turn straw into gold?
    - How is gold made? (Research in encyclopedia.)
    - Could the story have really happened?
    - What if the messenger hadn't overheard Rumpelstiltskin?

2. Rumpelstiltskin was an expert at turning straw into gold, so he was able to help the Miller's daughter. Have the students name some things they do so well that they could help someone else. Write a chart: Jennifer is great at kickball, Joshua is great at making nachos. Make a class book, entitled, "We Are Great At..." Have each student write and illustrate a page.

3. Have the students brainstorm some different endings to the story. Use a tape recorder to record your results. Listen to all the different endings.

4. Create your own chants. Write them on charts and chant frequently. Sentence strips can be made for visual matching or sequencing. Words can be written on cards to be put in order on a wall or pocket chart.

    Example: That funny little man
                 Turned straw into gold
                 Turned straw into gold
                 Turned straw into gold
                 That funny little man
                 Turned straw into gold
                 To help the Miller's daughter.

                 How did he turn that
                 Straw into gold
                 Straw into gold
                 Straw into gold
                 How did he do that
                 Straw into gold
                 To help the Miller's daughter.

54

55

Rumpelstiltskin/Baby

T.S. Denison & Co., Inc.   58   Story Masks for Fairy Tales

The Elves and the Shoemaker
Teacher's Guide

Exploring the Story

1. Discussion starters:
    • What did the Elves do when they came at night?
    • Why did the Shoemaker and his wife hide one night?
    • Why did the Shoemaker and his wife leave clothes for the elves?

2. What are elves like? Discuss and record ideas on a chart to read and reread.

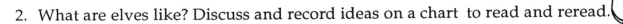

Elves _are tiny_ .

Elves _look funny_ .

Elves _work hard_ .

Elves _dance_ .

Elves _sing_ .

Elves _are magic_ .

Elves _have big ears_ .

Elves _wear funny hats_ .

Elves _wear funny shoes_ .

3. Write a book entitled, "If I Were An Elf..."

4. Pretend you are the Elves in this story and write a thank-you note to the shoemaker and his wife for the lovely clothes they left you. When you are Sinished with the Elves' thank-you note, pretend you are the Shoemaker and write a thank-you note to the Elves for making the shoes.
    Use notepaper or decorate some of your own.

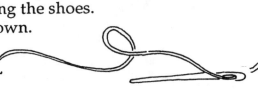

Create your own chants. Write them on charts and chant frequently. Sentence strips can be made for visual matching or sequencing. Words can be written on cards to be put in order on a wall or pocket chart.

Example:

The itty, bitty Elves made beautiful shoes,
The itty, bitty Elves made beautiful shoes,
The itty, bitty Elves made beautiful shoes,
To help the Shoemaker and his wife.

The itty, bitty Elves got brand new clothes,
The itty, bitty Elves got brand new clothes,
The itty, bitty Elves got brand new clothes,
With thanks from the Shoemaker and his wife.

63

Story Masks for Fairy Tales

65

66

The Gingerbread man
Teacher's Guide

Exploring the story

1. Discussion starters:
   - Why did the Gingerbread man run away?
   - Where was he going to go?
   - How could he talk since he was a cookie?
   - How many characters were chasing the Gingerbread Man?
   - Why didn't the characters chasing the Gingerbread Man eat him?
   - How did the fox succeed in eating him?
   - What does the expression "sly as a fox" mean?

2. Discuss with the students:
   - How do you think gingerbread cookies are made?
   - What ingredients are used?
   - What steps are taken?
   - Record responses and write the class "recipe" on a chart for future use.

3. Bake real gingerbread cookies. Write the recipe on posterboard for ease in reading. (Punch holes on top of the posterboard and add to your classroom cookbook. If you are not already keeping a "big book" of classroom recipes, this is a great activity to begin your classroom recipe book.) Read the recipe carefully with your students and compare it to the recipe that the children came up with in Activity 2.

4. Write the refrain on a wall chart for easy reference in choral reading. These same phrases can be written on sentence strips for visual matching or sequencing. The words from the refrain can be written on cards for the students to put in order in a wall or pocket chart.

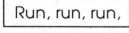 

| Run, run, run, |
| As fast as you can. |
| You can't catch me, |
| I'm the Gingerbread Man! |

5. Use the refrain to create other chants:

Hop, hop, hop,
As high as you can.
You can't catch me,
I'm the Gingerbread Man!

Jump, jump, jump,
As far as you can.
You can't catch me,
I'm the Gingerbread Man!

Skip, skip, skip,
As far as you can.
You can't catch me,
I'm the Gingerbread Man!

6. Encourage the students to write their own version of *The Gingerbread Man* or woman. They can have animals of their choice chase them or vary the ending of the story. A gingerbread cookie shape has been provided on the following page for those who would like to make a shape book. Each page of the book and cover are cut into the same shape.

7. Visit a bakery that makes gingerbread cookies.

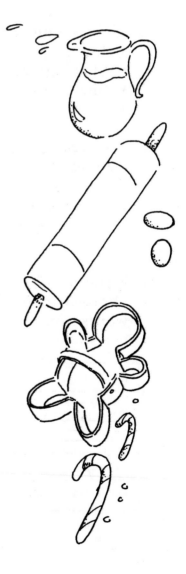

GINGERBREAD SHAPE BOOK PATTERN

73

74

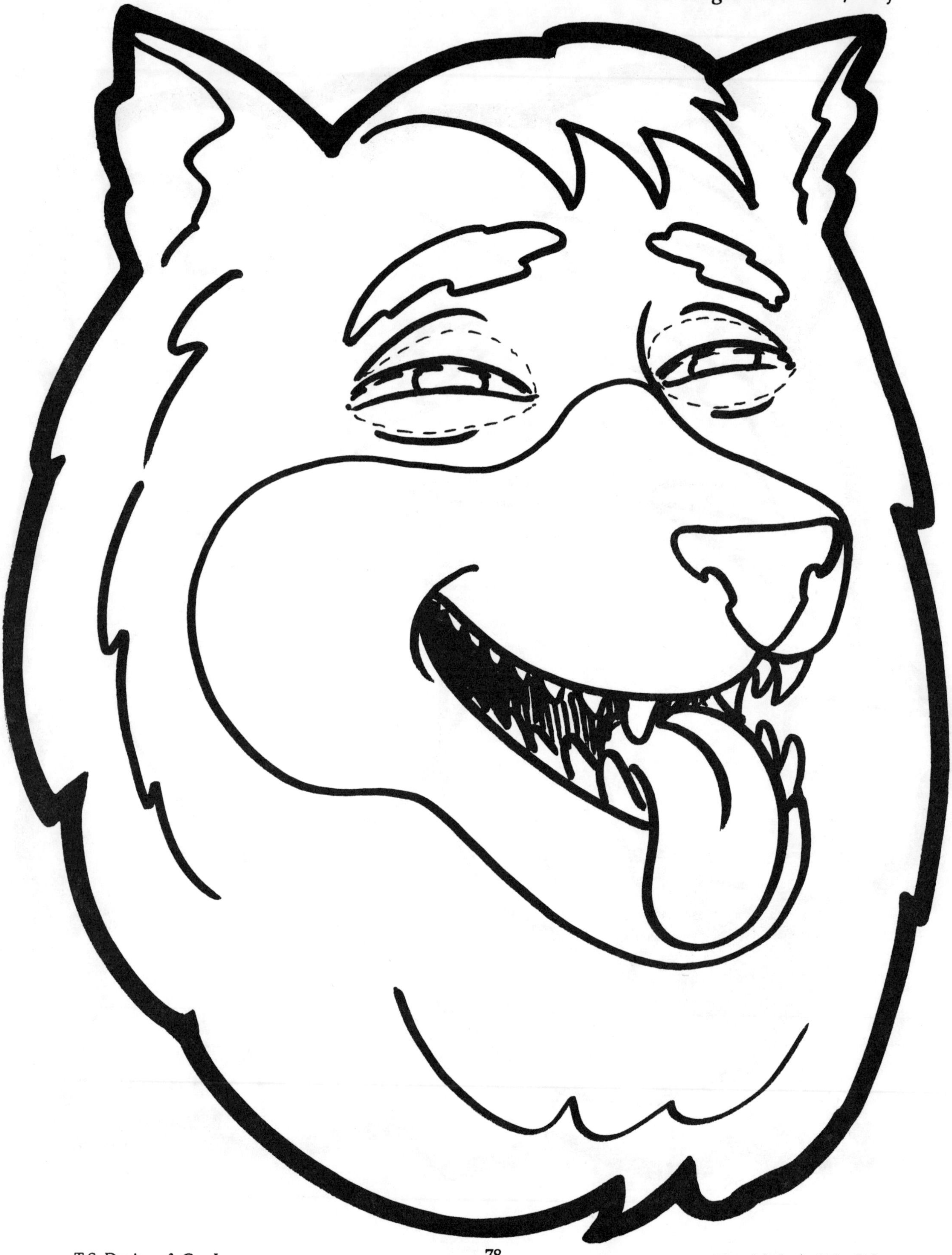

Red Riding Hood
Teacher's Guide

Exploring the Story

1. Discussion starters:
   - Why did Red Riding Hood go to Grandmother's house?
   - What did the Wolf want from Red Riding Hood?
   - How did the Wolf trick Red Riding Hood?

2. Compare this story of *Red Riding Hood* to the Chinese version of Red Riding Hood, *Lon Po-Po.* How are they similar? How are they different? Which version of the story do you like the best?

3. Create your own chants or choral reading verses. Write them on strips and chant frequently. Sentence strips can be made for visual matching or sequencing. Words can be written on cards to be put in order on a wall or pocket chart.

   Example: Group 1: Why, Grandmother, why are you eyes so large?
   Group 2: All the better to see you my dear!

   Group 1: Why, Grandmother, why are your ears so large?
   Group 2: All the better to hear you my dear!

   Group 1: Why, Grandmother, why are your teeth so large?
   Group 2: All the better to eat you my dear!

   Everyone: And they ran and they ran and they ran!

   (The childen will enjoy coming up with their own verses.)

| Why, Grandmother, why are your ears so large? |
| All the better to hear you my dear! |

| Why | , | Grandmother | , | why | are | your | ears | so | large | ? |
| All | the | better | to | hear | you | my | dear | ! | | |

4. In many children's stories, the wolf is a "bad" character. The wolf is most often portrayed as an animal that can do is mean and is only interested in harming other people or animals. Do some classroom research about "real" wolves. What are some of the traits of a real wolf that are "good." How are "real" wolves different from the wolves that we read about in children's story books? Make a large chart and record the differences.

5. Red Riding Hood's basket of "goodies" was by her side and saw everything that happened. The basket was with Red Riding Hood at her house, as Red Riding Hood walked through the forest, and watched everything that happened at Grandmother's house. If you were a magic, talking basket, what would you have told Red Riding Hood? Write a short story entitled, "Listen to me, Red Riding Hood." Write your story in a shape book. The following pattern is provided for you.

**RED RIDING HOOD'S BASKET,
SHAPE BOOK PATTERN**

82

83

84

87